Life as a
Chicken

Vic Parker

Heinemann
LIBRARY

Little Nippers

www.heinemann.co.uk/library
Visit our website to find out more information about **Heinemann Library** books.

To order:
☎ Phone 44 (0) 1865 888066
▤ Send a fax to 44 (0) 1865 314091
▭ Visit the Heinemann Bookshop at www.heinemann.co.uk/library to browse our
catalogue and order online.

First published in Great Britain by Heinemann
Library, Halley Court, Jordan Hill, Oxford
OX2 8EJ, part of Harcourt Education.
Heinemann is a registered trademark of Harcourt
Education Ltd.

Editorial: Jilly Attwood and Claire Throp
Design: Jo Hinton-Malivoire and bigtop,
Bicester, UK
Models made by: Jo Brooker
Picture Research: Catherine Bevan
Production: Séverine Ribierre

Originated by Dot Gradations
Printed and bound in China by South China
Printing Company

ISBN 0 431 17103 3 (hardback)
07 06 05 04 03
10 9 8 7 6 5 4 3 2 1

ISBN 0 431 17108 4 (paperback)
07 06 05 04 03
10 9 8 7 6 5 4 3 2 1

British Library Cataloguing in Publication Data
Parker, Vic
Life as a chicken
598.6'25
A full catalogue record for this book is available
from the British Library.

Acknowledgements
The publishers would like to thank the following
for permission to reproduce photographs:
Ardea p. **16**; Ardea pp. **22**, **23** (John Daniels);
Bruce Coleman pp. **4**, **11** (Jane Burton), **14**, **15**
(Robert Maier); Corbis p. **6**; FLPA p. **13** (Roger
Wilmshurst); Nature Picture Library p. **18**
(William Osborn); NHPA p. **19**; NHPA p. **10**
(G I Bernard); Oxford Scientific Films pp. **20**, **21**;
OSF pp. **8** (Martyn Chillmaid), **12** (Tony Allen);
Woodfall Wild Images p. **17** (E A Janes).

Cover photograph reproduced with permission of
Ardea/John Daniels

The publishers would like to thank Annie Davy
for her assistance in the preparation of this book.

Contents

Guess who?

Who has laid this nest of eggs?

A hen!

The hen sits on her eggs to keep them warm.

She gets up now and then to turn her eggs over.

Tap! tap! tap!

After 21 days a tiny Tap! Tap! Tap! comes from inside the eggs.

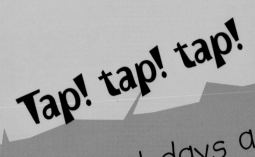

8

Cracks appear on the shells and out hatch ...

Hello chicks!

The chicks open their eyes and dry off.

They are covered all over with soft down.

Into the wide world

Soon the fuzzy, fluffy chicks
go for their first walk.

seeds to eat

From chick to chicken

When the chicks are a month old they begin to grow feathers.

Young male chickens are called cockerels.
Young female chickens are called pullets.

cockerel

pullet

Roaming free

During the day, the chickens walk
and **Squawk** around the farm.

At night, they sleep
tight in a chicken shed.

19

Eggs for eating

If female chickens are kept apart from male chickens, their eggs will not grow into chicks.

If they all live together, their eggs will hatch into ...

Count the chicks

... Lots of new chicks!

Index

The end

Notes for adults

The **Life as a . . .** series looks at the life cycles of familiar animals and plants, introducing the young child to the concept of change over time. There are four titles in the series and, when used together, they will enable comparison of similarities and differences between life cycles. The key curriculum early learning goals relevant to this series are:

Knowledge and understanding of the world
  – find out about, and identify, some features of living things that the young child observes
  – ask questions about why things happen
  – differentiate between past and present.

This book takes the reader on a circular journey from the beginning of a chicken's life as an egg, through its developmental stages (including where the chicken lives and what it needs to grow), to maturity and reproduction. The book will help children extend their vocabulary, as they will hear new words such as *down* (for the chicks' fluffy coats), *pullet* and *cockerel*. You might like to introduce the word *comb* when looking at the picture of the cockerel. The book explains that if pullets are kept apart from cockerels, their eggs will not grow into chicks. It may be helpful for young readers if you emphasize that the eggs we eat are the type that will never grow into chicks.

Additional information about chickens

Chickens are domestic birds – this means that they are kept and bred by humans for eating. There are approximately 150 different breeds of chicken in the world today. All chickens are descended from a type of pheasant found in the jungles of Southeast Asia. Chickens were first domesticated about 8000 years ago. A hen can lay about 250 eggs a year.

Follow-up activities

• Visit a children's farm to observe hens and chicks, pullets and cockerels.
• Hard-boil an egg and paint its shell.
• Make a model of a chicken using different materials such as clay or plasticine.